Developing
Professional Skills:
CONTRACTS

Debora L. Threedy
Lee E. Teitelbaum Professor of Law
S. J. Quinney College of Law
University of Utah

Adam H. Miller
2012 Quinney Fellow
S.J. Quinney College of Law
University of Utah

Series Editor
Colleen Medill

D1294634

WEST®

© 2013 West Academic Publishing
610 Opperman Drive
St. Paul, MN 55123
1-800-313-9378

West, West Academic Publishing, and West Academic are trademarks of West Publishing Corporation, used under license.

Printed in the United States of America

MAT #41231020
ISBN: 978-0-314-27954-5

This book is dedicated to the generations of law students
who have enriched my life; I hope I have taught
them at least as much as I have learned from them.
—D.L.T.

Preface

OVER THE NEARLY THIRTY YEARS I have been teaching law, the enterprise of legal education has been the subject of ongoing criticism. While that criticism takes many forms, two points have always struck me as crucial to any significant reform. The first criticism is that legal education, particularly in the first year, fails to provide regular formative assessments and thus fails to provide students with timely and effective feedback. The second criticism is that legal education, particularly in the first year, focuses primarily on doctrine, specifically on the transfer of knowledge about the substance of legal rules, and thus fails to provide students with experiential learning opportunities for applying that doctrine to solve legal problems. (As an aside, given how many contracts each one of us encounters in daily life, the fact that many if not most students can graduate from law school without knowing the first thing about drafting an agreement is mind-boggling.)

In the last few years I have been engaged in a quest to provide teaching materials to address these two criticisms. Along with colleagues at the Center for Innovation in Legal Education at the University of Utah's S. J. Quinney College of Law, I am in the process of developing a series of online videos with online assessments for use in first year classes. Please check on our progress at *www.TheFirstYear.org*. The idea behind these videos is that, given the large size of most first year classes, the most efficient way for professors to give students feedback on their mastery of the legal rules is through online media.

Having moved the doctrinal lectures and assessments online, time is then freed up in class for experiential learning activities, such as role plays, drafting exercises, and group projects. That is where this book and the others in the Developing Professional Skills series come in. It can be time-consuming to develop the materials for experiential learning activities from scratch. This book is made up of ten problems that provide professors and students with the raw materials for such activities. Each problem requires the students to do something: advise a client, negotiate a contract provision, prepare a term sheet, or draft a part of a contract or a litigation document. The idea behind these exercises is that deep learning and mastery can only occur when students actually use the doctrine they've learned to solve problems.

Several individuals and organizations have contributed to this book. The chronologically first one is Professor Colleen Medill who recruited me to participate in the series. The first in terms of the volume of his contributions is my co-author, Adam H. Miller. Adam was a second year law student when he was assigned to me as a Quinney Fellow to assist in the research and preparation of this book. He enthusiastically took the laboring oar in drafting the exercises and I am delighted to share authorship with him. I would also like to acknowledge Professor Tina Stark's contributions to the project of teaching contract drafting. She has been a generous mentor to professors like me who decide that it is time to move beyond doctrine and into praxis in the classroom. Personally, I also owe a debt of gratitude to Professor Tom Haney, in whose Contracts class I first discovered that this was an area of law I found congenial, and to my father, who among many other gifts, first introduced me to the practice of law. Finally, I would like to thank the S. J. Quinney College of Law for its support of this project and to the editorial staff for their assistance in bringing it to the page.

Debora L. Threedy
July 1, 2013

Introduction

Developing Professional Skills: Contracts provides an opportunity to begin developing the skills essential to the practice of law. Law school tends to focus on the legal analytical skills of determining "the law" and arriving at answers to legal questions. Each chapter in this book allows you the opportunity to apply that analysis to scenarios involving client interaction, with the goal of developing the equally important skills of counseling, negotiating, advocating, and drafting.

The chapters in this book cover topics common to first year contracts courses. Chapter One asks you to draft an e-mail to a client concerning the elements of contract formation. Chapter Two requires you to draft a demand letter on behalf of a client who relied on assurances that an ultimate contract was inevitable. In Chapter Three, you will prepare for a client interview concerning a disagreement about an oral contract to purchase goods. Chapter Four asks you to negotiate the non-compete clause of an employment agreement. In Chapter Five, you will draft the language of a sales contract to avoid a potentially misleading representation. Chapter Six allows an opportunity to advocate to the court regarding the admissibility of an oral side agreement to a written contract. Chapter Seven asks you to advise both parties to a transaction on the purpose and limits of express conditions. In Chapter Eight, a client requests your help in renegotiating a land lease when the circumstances change. Chapter Nine asks you to redraft contract language to clarify a standard form contract. Finally, Chapter Ten provides a capstone project, requiring you to counsel a client about possible outcomes to a business deal gone wrong, prepare a complaint, negotiate a settlement, and draft a release of liability.

The skills addressed in each chapter—client counseling, advocacy, negotiating, and legal drafting—are the central skills of the legal profession. *Developing Professional Skills: Contracts* will expose you to these concepts and provide the opportunity to begin developing these skills.

Enjoy.

— Debora Threedy and Adam Miller

Table of Contents

Chapter 1: Prerequisites for a Contract   1
- *Theater Companies Acting-up*
  Skill: Client Counseling

Chapter 2: Reliance on a Promise   7
- *Smart Solutions*
  Skill: Advocacy

Chapter 3: Whether a Writing is Necessary   13
- *Puppy Delight*
  Skill: Client Counseling

Chapter 4: Public Policy Constraints on Private Agreements   19
- *A Dental Dilemma*
  Skill: Negotiation

Chapter 5: Representations and Misrepresentations   27
- *Counting Clients*
  Skill: Drafting

Chapter 6: The Admissibility of Extrinsic Evidence   37
- *A Fowl Contract?*
  Skill: Advocacy

Chapter 7: Conditions v. Covenants   47
- *Wicks and Only Wicks*
  Skill: Client Counseling

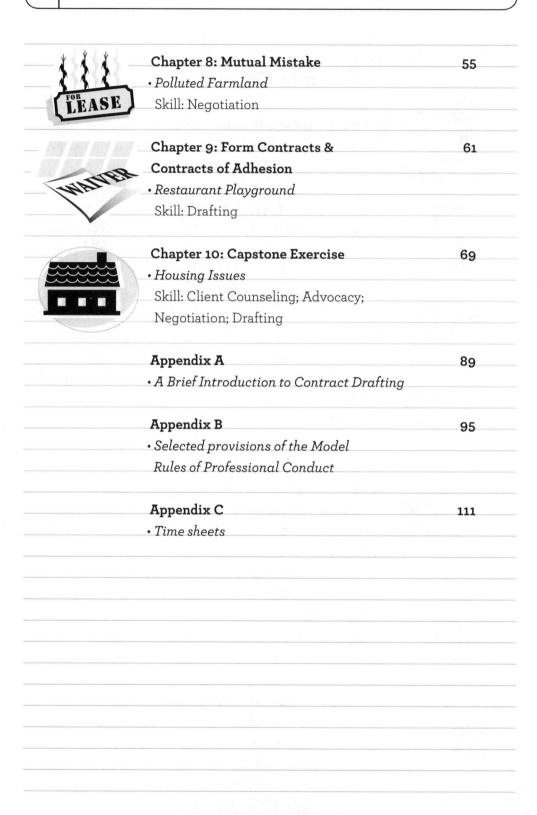

Chapter 8: Mutual Mistake   55
• *Polluted Farmland*
  Skill: Negotiation

Chapter 9: Form Contracts &   61
Contracts of Adhesion
• *Restaurant Playground*
  Skill: Drafting

Chapter 10: Capstone Exercise   69
• *Housing Issues*
  Skill: Client Counseling; Advocacy;
  Negotiation; Drafting

Appendix A   89
• *A Brief Introduction to Contract Drafting*

Appendix B   95
• *Selected provisions of the Model*
Rules of Professional Conduct

Appendix C   111
• *Time sheets*

Developing Professional Skills:
CONTRACTS

CHAPTER ONE

Prerequisites for a Contract
Theater Companies Acting-up

YOU ARE A NEW ASSOCIATE at a well-respected law firm and you just received the following email from the managing partner:

To: [Your name]
From: David Bradley
Subject: Assignment, ASAP
Date: [Today's date]

Dear New Associate:

A belated welcome to the firm! I am a long-time board member for the non-profit "Noble Theater Company." Aside from raising donations, I provide counsel as needed.

Trent Block, Noble's director, called me at home this morning concerning a contract issue that needs immediate attention. Trent was approached a couple of weeks ago by Eva Strong, owner of the newly formed "Puppets & People Theater." Eva asked to borrow a set of Trent's pioneer costumes for a production. Although Eva offered to pay a rental fee, he told her she could have the costumes for free. Trent said another theater company helped him get started, and he wanted to help. He did ask Eva to return the costumes in the same condition as when she borrowed them.

Anyways, Eva returned the costumes dirty—the actors sweat all over them. Trent told Eva the costumes needed to be dry-cleaned because they would be ruined if they were stored dirty. Eva said she knew that, but hadn't realized it would cost nearly $5,000 to have all the custom outfits cleaned. She didn't want to pay. Trent asked me if he could enforce their contract and have Eva pay for the dry-cleaning.

I am off to have lunch with the Governor and need you to email a response to Trent@NobleTheater.org. Trent expects a response this afternoon, so please take care of this ASAP. Although this will be pro bono work, I'll need you to turn in a timesheet, as we report the amount of pro bono work we donate each year. Client is Noble Theater Company, # 37785PB.

David P. Bradley, esq.
Managing Partner
Workhard & Longe

Prepare an email response to the client's question. Limit your analysis to 200 words.

 ## Points to Consider:

(1) What are the required elements of a contract? Have they been satisfied?

(2) What tone should your email take? How will you address the issues of law and a recommendation?

(3) How will you deal with the fact that you have only heard one side of the situation?

Email Form

To: Trent@NobleTheatre.org
From: [your name]@WLlaw.com
Subject: Costume Dry-cleaning
Date: [Today's date]

Dear Mr. Block,

Please contact me if you have any additional questions.

Very truly yours,
[Your name]

Time Sheet

Attorney:

Client:

Billing No.

DATE	DESCRIPTION	TIME

CHAPTER TWO

Reliance on a Promise
Smart Solutions

FOR YEARS, your firm has represented Peter Janowski in his various successful business start-ups. *Smart Solutions,* Peter's latest company, aims to provide an easy and inexpensive way to replace cracked smartphone touchscreens. Peter plans to provide a drop-box inside each branch of a nationwide box store. His employees will construct and install the drop-boxes. They will also empty the drop-boxes and return repaired phones to the customer within a day. Peter pitched his idea to several major smart phone retailers, receiving the most positive response from the CEO of *Electronics Supercity,* Jen Walters. In a March meeting, Jen told Peter that she wanted *Smart Solutions* drop-boxes only in *Electronics Supercity* stores and Peter said he would have a draft agreement prepared for her attorneys to review.

You helped draft Peter's initial agreement and provided it to Jen at the end of March. Jen responded by email:

From:	Jen Walters (jen@ElectronicsSupercity.com)
To:	Peter Janowski (Peter@SmartSolutions.com)
Subject:	Cell phone screen replacement drop-boxes
Date:	April 3

Peter,
Thank you for preparing that agreement so quickly. My attorneys are making some minor revisions but we are on the same page. Again, I want these drop-boxes exclusively in our stores.

We will be in touch shortly, Jen

Peter ceased negotiating with other retailers and by the end of April, secured contracts with the three largest smartphone makers to purchase replacement screens, guaranteeing each maker he would purchase at least $100,000 worth of screens in the first year. In a phone conversation on May 1, Jen informed Peter her attorneys approved the contract without significant modifications and that she needed to obtain the approval of the board of directors before she could return it to him, but not to worry because she ran the board. She said the board was meeting the following week and that she wanted to have the drop-boxes installed by early summer.

Peter leased office and shop spaces in 16 cities around the country and began hiring staff. He also contracted to have the drop-boxes constructed and advertising produced. He attempted contacting Jen several times throughout the month but was only able to leave messages with her secretary. Peter came to speak with you upon receiving the following email:

From:	Jen Walters (jen@ElectronicsSupercity.com)
To:	Peter Janowski (Peter@SmartSolutions.com)
Subject:	re: Cell phone screen replacement drop-boxes
Date:	June 1

Peter,

Electronics Supercity has decided to develop our own electronics repair division and will not need the services of Smart Solutions.

Thank you for your consideration,
Jen

Peter believes his business will fail without this contract. He has learned that the other box stores have already contracted with his competitors and he cannot back out of his leases or agreements with the cell phone makers. He estimates he has spent about $200,000 since first speaking with Jen. Worse, he purchased a yacht with a portion of his anticipated profits, estimated at $50,000 the first year and well over a million dollars within five years.

Peter has asked you to draft a demand letter to *Electronics Supercity*. Do not spend more than an hour or two on the draft.

 ## Points to Consider:

(1) Does a contract exist?

(2) Can Peter rely on Promissory Estoppel? Compare with cases you have read.

(3) What can Peter demand? Performance? Losses? Expected profits?

Demand Letter

Law Office of Abbott and Associates

1200 Center St.,

Anywhere, Blackacre

June 8, 20___

Jen Walters

Chief Executive Officer

Electronics Supercity

789 Midtown Way, Whiteacre

Ms. Walters:

Very truly yours,

[Your name]

CHAPTER THREE

Whether a Writing Is Necessary
Puppy Delight

YOUR SECRETARY FORWARDED the following emails and notified you Susan Espinoza, a potential new client, would be in to speak with you in an hour. Review the available information and prepare discussion points and relevant questions on the attached initial client interview form.

From:	Espinoza@petworld.com
To:	[Your name]@lawUSA.com
Subject:	I need help!
Date:	Sept. 15 @ 10:00 am

I need a new attorney, and I hear you are the best. I own and manage PetWorld, you've seen them all over town. Lots of people get puppies in the Spring, so I sell a lot of puppy food.

I ordered 500 bags over the phone from Dave at PuppyDelight, but when he emailed the receipt, it said I purchased 700 bags.

I let him know he made an error but 700 bags were delivered and I rejected the whole delivery. Dave left a message on my phone this morning asking me to call him. He didn't sound happy. I'm not dealing with that incompetent company anymore. Besides, I never signed anything so I'm not paying for it.

I attached the emails below. I will be in to talk with you in an hour.

— Susan Espinoza

From: Dave@puppydelight.com
To: Espinoza@petworld.com
Subject: PuppyDelight Order
Date: August 30 @ 7:32 am

Ms. Espinoza – here is your purchase order receipt.
Thanks again, Dave

Voted "best puppy food" worldwide

PURCHASE ORDER No.:

SOLD TO: Susan Espinoza	
700 bags of Puppy Delight	$12.00/bg
TOTAL	$8,400.00

Thank You & Order Again!

Points to Consider:

(1)   What body of law applies to this transaction, common law or statutory?

(2)   Does the statute of frauds apply? Is there a writing that satisfies the statute? Do any exceptions apply?

(3)   Are there are non-legal questions you may want to go over with Ms. Connor? For example, why is she looking for a new attorney?

Initial Client Interview Form

Attorney:

Date:

Regarding:

Conflicts Check: ___ No conflicts   **Engagement Letter:**

                ___ Approved despite conflict   ___ Submitted

                ___ Representation declined   ___ Signed

Client Information

Name:

Billing Address:

Contact Address:

Email:

Phone:

Client Goals

Points of Discussion

To Do

CHAPTER FOUR

Public Policy Constraints on Private Agreements
A Dental Dilemma

CENTERVILLE IS A SMALL suburban town, located directly between two larger cities. Fifty miles to the north is Northford and fifty miles to the south is Southland. Dr. Watson has served the residents of Centerville for over thirty years as the only dentist in town, but has recently been thinking about retiring to the Caribbean. Dr. Watson wants to bring on a young partner who will gradually buy out his dental practice over the next five years. Following an extensive search for a trustworthy partner, Dr. Watson has tentatively settled on Dr. Price. However, Dr. Watson remains concerned about investing time and money into training a new dentist, only to have that dentist open a competing practice next door.

Originally from the Centerville area, Dr. Price is graduating dental school this coming spring at the top of his class. Dr. Price wants a mentor to teach him how to run a practice, bill clients, and hire staff. He has several lucrative offers to work as an employee in other cities, but prefers to establish or purchase a practice near his hometown. However, recognizing this is his first job out of dental school, Dr. Price is concerned about limiting his future options in case the partnership does not work out.

The two dentists get along well, genuinely like each other, and are optimistic about their business future together. Wisely, both

Dr. Watson and Dr. Price hired counsel to draft their partnership agreement, terms of purchase, and salary. The last unresolved issue is the provisions of a non-com-pete clause (also called a covenant not to compete) between the two parties. With this provision, Dr. Price would promise not to open a competing practice in the event the partnership with Dr. Watson did not work out.

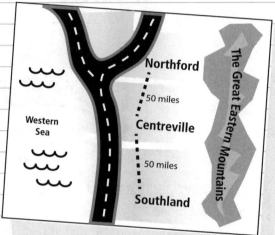

You represent either Dr. Watson or Dr. Price, while a fellow classmate represents the other party. Your goal is to negotiate the non-compete clause to meet your client's needs. Your professor will provide you with additional information relevant to your client's interests and you should read over the supplement on theories of negotiation. After the negotiation, memorialize the agreed terms on the checklist provided. If you are unable to agree on terms, you and the opposing counsel are to jointly draft and sign a letter to your clients, describing the negotiation process and stating why you are unable to agree.

Points to Consider:

(1) What is the purpose of a non-compete clause? Whose interests is it meant to protect? What public policy is served by such clauses?

(2) How will you approach your negotiation? Will you best achieve your client's goals by being combative or collaborative?

(3) What is included in the covenant not to compete? What conduct does it prohibit? What conduct does it allow?

(4) Public policy generally requires non-compete clauses to be reasonably limited temporally and geographically. Would the clause you have negotiated survive a challenge in court?

Non-Compete Checklist

Actions/conduct prohibited:

Actions/conduct allowed (if any):

Geographic limits:

Temporal limits:

Remedies for failure to comply:

> **SUPPLEMENTAL**: **Negotiation Theory**

There are two primary types of bargaining. In positional bargaining, the parties view the negotiation as a zero sum game where one party's gain is equivalent to the other party's loss. In interest-based bargaining, the parties view the negotiation as a problem-solving process rather than a zero sum game. The parties are perceived to have complementary or mutual interests, so that bargaining may result in overall gains for both sides.

In positional bargaining, each party typically starts the negotiation from an extreme position (high or low rent, for example). The parties expect that small concessions gradually will be made by each side until a moderate or middle ground outcome is reached. Bluffing and puffing is common as the parties negotiate. When an attorney negotiates on behalf of a client, however, lying is prohibited as a violation of the lawyer's professional responsibilities under Rule 4.1 of the Model Rules of Professional Conduct.

Common strategies used in positional bargaining are:
    (1) make the other side offer first;
    (2) make the other side compromise first;
    (3) claim a lack of authority to do what the other side requests;
    (4) act irrationally; and
    (5) claim the other side is irrational or making unreasonable demands.

In interest-based bargaining, each party focuses on the problem to be solved and tries to identify at least one area of common interest where mutual gains may be achieved. Creative solutions are used to accommodate the goals and objectives of the parties.

Common strategies used in interest-based bargaining are:
    (1) focus on the problem, not the people or their personalities;
    (2) focus on the mutual interests of the parties, not on fixed demands or positions;
    (3) emphasize points of collaboration, not confrontation; and
    (4) empathize with the needs of the other side.

Depending on the circumstances, lawyers who are effective negotiators often use a combination of positional and interest-based bargaining to achieve the best result for their clients.

From: Colleen E. Medill, *Developing Professional Skills: Property* 47 (2012).

CHAPTER FIVE

Representations and Misrepresentations

Counting Clients

YOUR SUPERVISING ATTORNEY has asked you to review
Article 3 of an acquisition agreement for the firm's client, Valley
Communications, a local landline Internet service provider.
Valley Communications services a community of roughly 50,000
homes and businesses in an economically thriving area of your
state. Your client is in negotiations to sell the business to WorldNet,
a large national company. Your firm drafted an extensive acquisition
agreement and a partner asked you to review the representations
and warranties with your client to verify accuracy.

The following portions of the draft include the introductory sections of
the contract, the subject matter, consideration and closing provisions,
and the article containing some of the representations and warranties
that you have been asked to review:

DRAFT

ACQUISITION AGREEMENT

This **Acquisition Agreement**, dated _____, 20___, is between Valley Communications, Inc., a Utah corporation ("Valley"), and WorldNet, Inc., a Delaware corporation ("WN").

Background

This Agreement provides for WN's purchase of substantially all of Valley's assets.

The parties agree as follows:

Article 1: Definitions

[Article I consists of the Definitions used in the Agreement and has been omitted.]

Article 2: Purchase and Sale

2.1. Purchase and Sale of Assets. At the Closing, Valley shall sell and WN shall purchase the Assets.

2.2. Purchase Price. The purchase price is $_____.

2.3. Closing. The Closing is to take place at the offices of Workhard and Longe LLP, 123 Main St., Anywhere, Blackacre on the Closing Date, or on another date and time agreed upon by the parties.

2.4. Closing Deliveries.

[This section sets out what each party is required to produce at the Closing in order for the transaction to be consummated. Typically, this includes items like deeds, stock certificates, subsidiary agreements, and proof of funds transfer.]

Article 3: Valley's Representations and Warranties

Valley represents and warrants to WN as follows:

3.1. Organization. Valley is a corporation duly organized, validly existing, and in good standing under the laws of Utah.

3.2. Corporate Power and Authority. Valley has all necessary corporate power and authority to own and operate its Assets and to carry on its business; and to sign and perform this Agreement.

3.3. Authorization. Valley has taken all necessary corporate action to authorize the signing and performance of this Agreement.

3.4 Enforceability. The Agreement has been duly signed by Valley and constitutes its legal, valid and binding obligation.

3.5. Financial Statements.

> **3.5.1. Audited Financial Statements.** Valley's balance sheets dated December 31, [previous year], and December 31, [two years prior], and all related financial statements, certified by Elder and Young, independent accountants, have been prepared according to generally accepted accounting principles and fairly present Valley's financial condition as of the date indicated.

> **3.5.2. Unaudited Financial Statements.** Valley's unaudited financial statements dated September 30, [current year], have been prepared according to generally accepted accounting principles and fairly present Valley's financial condition as of that date.

3.6. Title to Assets. Valley has good title to all of the Assets, except as noted in Schedule 7.

3.7. Customers.

> 3.7.1. **Previous Year.** Valley had 30,000 customers in calendar year [previous year].

> **3.7.2. Current Year.** Valley had 48,000 customers in the period between January 1, [current year], and September 30, [current year].

[Additional representations and warranties omitted.]

In response to your assignment, you send and receive the following emails:

From: [your.name]@WLlaw.com
To: natsuki@valleycommunications.net
Subject: Inquiry into client representation

Natsuki,

The Acquisition Agreement makes the following representation and warranty at 3.7.2: "Valley had 48,000 customers in the period between January 1, [current year], and September 30, [current year]."

This number seems high, considering there are only 50,000 residences and businesses in the entire area. For the purpose of accuracy, can you please explain how you reached this number?

From: natsuki@valleycommunications.net
To: [your.name]@WLlaw.com
Subject: re: Inquiry into client representation

Thanks for your inquiry. We did have 48,000 contracts last year. We started the year with 30,000 customers but lost about half of them when Cheapo-Net moved into town in February. When Cheapo-Net folded in June, we had a surge of clients returning, roughly equaling the number that left in February. Presumably, these were the same clients, but I can't be sure. We also signed up 3,000 more clients than we lost throughout the remainder of the year. That's the total: 48,000.

I can see how the claim in 3.7.2 could be slightly misleading. We only currently have 33,000 total clients. I fear WorldNet would back out of the deal if we change the number. We need to send the contract over to WorldNet today. Can you provide alternative versions of 3.7.2 that are more accurate without changing the number 48,000, and let me know why your versions are better?

Your assignment is to re-draft Paragraph 3.7.2 so that it is accurate, along with a brief email to the client explaining why you chose that language or, alternatively, explaining why it is not possible to use the figure 48,000.

 Points to Consider:

(1) What does the heading "Representations and Warranties" indicate? (See Appendix A)

(2) Do you think there is an ethical requirement to verify the original representation and warranty made in 3.7.2 if you are aware the number appears high? Why or why not?

(3) How would you respond if the client insisted on using 3.7.2 as is?

Re-draft of Paragraph 3.7

3.7. Customers.

    3.7.1. Previous Year. Valley had 30,000 customers in calendar year [previous year].

    3.7.2. Current Year.

Email to Client

From: [your.name]@WLlaw.com
To: natsuki@valleycommunications.net
Subject: re: Inquiry into client representation

CHAPTER SIX

The Admissibility of Extrinsic Evidence
A Fowl Contract?

FARMER STAN HATCH usually sells his chickens to a large factory down south for about $5 each. The company purchasing his flock hires a transportation company and observes the industry custom of paying Hatch only for the chickens arriving alive. Occasionally, the truck breaks down or crashes, but Hatch takes out insurance to guard against any major loss.

This year, Hatch has changed his business model and is trying to break into the local health food market, mortgaging the farm to raise a flock of organic, free-range chickens. He negotiated through the summer with two area butchers, finally agreeing to sell 1000 chickens for $15 each to Brock Bros. Butchers. The parties hand-wrote and signed the following:

> Stan Hatch agrees to sell 1000 organic, free-range chickens to Brock Bros. Butchers for $15 per chicken by the end of September, payment due within 30 days. The parties will hire Fowl Transport to ship the birds and split the delivery cost evenly.
>
> Date: August 29, 2013

Hatch loaded the birds onto the Fowl Transport truck, but the truck encountered a freak early fall snowstorm, killing half the birds. Brock Bros. sent Hatch payment in the amount of $7,300, representing $15 apiece for the birds that arrived alive, less half the transportation cost. Hatch called Mr. Brock to complain, saying he had chosen Brock Bros. because of their local reputation for paying for all birds shipped. He also said he did not purchase insurance for this delivery and is afraid he will not be able to make his mortgage payment, maybe even lose the farm. He threatened legal action.

Mr. Brock responded that they only paid for all birds shipped when dealing with long-term suppliers, and that with first time suppliers like Hatch they followed the industry custom of only paying for birds delivered alive.

Last week Brock Bros. was served with the following complaint:

Abbott & Associates
Thomas Abbott, Blackacre Bar # 6789
Attorney for Plaintiff Stan Hatch
1200 Center St.
Anywhere, Blackacre
tabbott@Abbottlaw.com
000-987-5432

FIRST DISTRICT COURT, WAYNE COUNTY
STATE OF BLACKACRE

Stan Hatch, an individual,	)	
Plaintiff	)	COMPLAINT
v.	)	
	)	Judge C. Wodford
Brock Bros. Butchers,	)	
a Blackacre Corporation,	)	No. 3164-193cv
Defendant.	)	

COMPLAINT

Plaintiff Stan Hatch complains of Defendant Brock Bros. Butchers, as follows:

JURISDICTION, VENUE & PARTIES

1. This Court has jurisdiction over this action pursuant to Blackacre Code § 24.34.5 (2006).

2. Venue of this action is properly placed with this court pursuant to Blackacre Code § 24.55.1 (2006).

3. Plaintiff Stan Hatch is an individual and resident of the State of Blackacre.

4. Defendant Brock Bros. Butchers is a Blackacre corporation with its principal place of business in Crescent City, Wayne County, Blackacre.

CAUSE OF ACTION
(Breach of Contract)

5.   On or about August 29, 2013, Plaintiff and Defendant entered into a contract for the sale and purchase of 1,000 free-range organic chickens at the price of $15.00 each.

6.   Defendant has a practice of paying for each bird consigned to Fowl Transport, regardless of the number of birds that arrive alive at the time of delivery.

7.   That practice was incorporated into the contract between Plaintiff and Defendant.

8.   Plaintiff performed his obligations under the contract by consigning 1,000 free-range chickens to a common carrier for delivery to Plaintiff.

9.   Through no fault of Plaintiff's, 500 chickens died during transport.

10. Defendant tendered Plaintiff a check for $7,300, representing payment for 500 chickens, less $200 or one-half of the transportation costs.

11. Defendant failed to perform its obligation to pay for each bird consigned and thus breached the contract.

12. As a result of Defendant's breach of the contract, Plaintiff has suffered damages, both direct and consequential.

THEREFORE, Plaintiff demands judgment against Defendant in the amount of Plaintiff's damages plus interest, costs and attorney's fees, and for such other relief as the court deems just.

Dated this 18th day of November, [current year]

Abbott & Associates

_____

Thomas Abbott
1200 Center St.
Anywhere, Blackacre
Attorney for Plaintiff

Brock Bros. Butchers has retained your firm to represent it in this litigation. The partner in your firm to whom the matter was assigned has determined that Brock Bros. should answer the complaint. Review the complaint and draft the answer. A template has been provided below for your use in answering the complaint. Do not spend more than an hour or two on drafting the Answer.

 Points to Consider:

(1) What allegations are necessary to state a claim for breach of contract? Does the complaint make the necessary allegations? If not, the defendant could make a motion to dismiss for failure to state a claim for relief, although in most jurisdictions the defendant can also raise the failure to state a claim as an affirmative defense.

(2) In general, a defendant that answers a complaint must choose from the following responses for each paragraph in the complaint:

- Admit the allegation(s) in the paragraph.

- Deny the allegation(s) in the paragraph.

- State that defendant lacks sufficient information to form a belief as to the truth of the allegation(s) in the paragraph.

- A combination of two or more of the preceding, such as admitting the allegation that [...] and denying the remainder of the allegations in the paragraph.

How should Brock Bros. answer each of the allegations?

(3) Are there any affirmative defenses Brock Bros. can raise?

Answer

[Your Name], Bar # 777
Workhard & Longe
Attorney for Defendant
123 Main St.
Anywhere, Blackacre
Your.name@WLlaw.com
000.123.4567

FIRST DISTRICT COURT, WAYNE COUNTY
STATE OF BLACKACRE

Stan Hatch, an individual,	)	
Plaintiff	)	COMPLAINT
v.	)	
	)	Judge C. Wodford
Brock Bros. Butchers,	)	
a Blackacre Corporation,	)	No. 3164-193cv
Defendant.	)	

ANSWER

Defendant Brock Bros. Butchers, by and through its attorney, answers the Complaint of Plaintiff Stan Hatch as follows:

1. Defendant admits the allegations in Paragraph 1 of the Complaint.

2. Defendant admits the allegations in Paragraph 2 of the Complaint.

3. Defendant _____ the allegations in Paragraph 3 of the Complaint.

4. Defendant admits the allegations in Paragraph 4 of the Complaint.

5. Defendant _____ the allegations in Paragraph 5 of the Complaint.

6. Defendant _____ the allegations in Paragraph 6 of the Complaint.

7. Defendant _____ the allegations in Paragraph 7 of the Complaint.
8. Defendant _____ the allegations in Paragraph 8 of the Complaint.
9. Defendant _____ the allegations in Paragraph 9 of the Complaint.
10. Defendant admits the allegations in Paragraph 10 of the Complaint.
11. Defendant _____ the allegations in Paragraph 11 of the Complaint.
12. Defendant _____ the allegations in Paragraph 12 of the Complaint.

Affirmative Defense [if more than one, number them]

For its [first] Affirmative Defense, Defendant alleges _____
[in the event that there are multiple allegations making up the affirmative defense, the sentence would continue] as follows:

1.
2. [etc.]

WHEREFORE Defendant requests that Plaintiff's Complaint be dismissed, with prejudice.

DATED this 12th day of December, 20___.

Workhard & Longe

_____
[Your Name], Bar # 777
123 Main St.
Anywhere, Blackacre
Attorney for Defendant

CHAPTER SEVEN

Conditions v. Covenants
Wicks and Only Wicks

THIS MORNING you received a phone call from Ms. Beth Rush.
She was a classmate of yours in law school. She successfully completed
her first year, but decided not to return after inheriting a substantial
fortune from her grandfather. She intends to build a ski chalet on the
slopes of his favorite ski mountain and has decided to write her own
construction contract.

Her grandfather's wealth came from selling the business he started
fifty years ago, *Wicks Wires*. The wire produced by *Wicks* is identical
to other brands, but Ms. Rush feels it would be poor taste to use her
grandfather's inheritance on a competitor's product. She wants to
ensure the contractor uses only *Wicks Wire* in her chalet.

Ms. Rush wants to speak with you because she is concerned the
contractor may be able to substitute another brand of wire. She recalls
Jacobs & Young v. Kent, a case she read in her contracts class. She also
thinks, that while you're at it, you should look over the rest of the contract and make suggestions.

She tells you that she will stop by this afternoon, along with the contractor, Caleb ManyHorses, to go over the contract. She emails you a copy of the draft contract and says you should rewrite the provision, if necessary, to ensure only *Wicks Wire* is used in her chalet. She also makes it clear that she does not want you to draft a new contract, "just give me suggestions on this one."

Prepare a memorandum in which you provide any suggestions you may have for revising the contract.

 Points to Consider:

(1) What are the limits of contract drafting? Can you guarantee how a court would interpret any provision?

(2) What might be other methods of accomplishing the same goal?

(3) Should courts enforce the exact language of a contract or allow for substantially similar performance?

(4) Note that both Ms. Rush and Mr. ManyHorses are going to be present: what ethical issues does that present? How should you manage them?

CONSTRUCTION CONTRACT

This **Construction Contract,** dated _____, 20___, is between Beth Rush ("Owner") and ManyHorses Construction LLC, a Whiteacre corporation ("Builder").

The parties agree as follows:

1. Builder's Obligation. Builder shall construct the ski chalet according to this Contract and the attached building Plans and Specifications.

2. Owner's Obligation. Owner shall pay Builder $300,000.00 in three equal payments.

3. Payment Schedule. The three payments are due and payable as follows:

　　a. Payment 1, within five business days of Contractor's completion of the site preparation, grading, and pouring of concrete slab.

　　b. Payment 2, within five business days of Builder's completion of the closing in of the house, including the installation of a roof, windows, doors, and siding.

　　c. Payment 3, within five business days of Builder's satisfactory completion of the ski chalet.

4. Construction Materials.

　　a. All building materials are to be new (unless otherwise specified).

　　b. Only Wicks Wires shall be installed in the ski chalet.

5. Change Orders. Both parties must agree to the specifics and price of any modifications, omissions, or additions to this agreement.

6. Warranties.

　　a. Builder warrants all work meets a professional standard, in accordance to all applicable laws and building codes.

　　b. Owner warrants she has the financial ability to pay, owns the property in fee simple absolute, and will obtain all required building permits.

7. Other.

    a. The Contract contains the entire understanding of the parties and all prior agreements and understandings are merged into this Contract.

    b. The parties may not transfer or assign this Agreement without the written agreement of the other party.

    c. The laws of Whiteacre govern the contract.

    d. If a court invalidates any portion of the Contract, all remaining provisions remain in effect.

By signature below, the parties have executed this Contract:

OWNER: Beth Rush

_____(sign), _____ (date)

BUILDER: Caleb ManyHorses

_____(sign), _____ (date)

Memorandum

MEMORANDUM

To:

From: [your name]

Re: Ski Chalet Construction Contract

Date:

CHAPTER EIGHT

Mutual Mistake
Polluted Farmland

FARMER STAN HATCH decided to expand his farming operations into growing organic corn. He approached the Farmland Holding Co. to locate and rent land to grow his new crop. Farmland Holding owns large tracts of rent-able farmland throughout the state and specializes in matching farmer needs with appropriate land. Farmer Stan told Farmland Holding he needs fifty acres of land within the county that could receive an organic certification. Organic certifications require the land to have been free of pesticides and other chemicals for a certain number of years.

Farmland Holding proposed a suitable plot of land. Farmer Stan and a representative from Farmland Holding inspected the site and then entered into the following agreement:

AGRICULTURAL LEASE

Agricultural Lease, dated July 1,[current year], between Farmland Holding Co., a corporation organized under the laws of Blackacre ("Landlord"), and Stan Hatch, an individual residing in Blackacre ("Tenant"),

<u>WITNESSETH</u>:

WHEREAS Tenant seeks acreage to operate an organic farm; and

WHEREAS Landlord has acreage suitable for organic farming available for lease;

NOW, THEREFORE, in consideration of the mutual promises set out below and other good and valuable consideration, the parties agree as follows:

1. Landlord shall lease the fifty acres located at the northwest corner of Rural Rd. and County St. in Winnebago County, Blackacre (the "Farmland") to Tenant for the period beginning on January 1, [current year], and ending five years afterwards on December 31, [five years after current year] (the "Term").

2. Tenant shall pay Landlord $1,000.00 per quarter in rent for the Farmland, due on the first day of January, April, July and October of each year during the Term.

3. Landlord represents and warrants that it has good title to the Farmland and that no other person has the right to occupy or use the Farmland for any purpose.

4. Landlord may enter the Farmland at any reasonable time (a) to consult with Tenant, (b) to make repairs or improvements, or (c) to develop mineral rights, subject to the condition that none of the above interferes with Tenant's ability to carry on normal farming operations.

5. Tenant shall use the Farmland solely for farming operations and shall not use any non-organic substances for pest control or fertilization on the Farmland.

6. If Tenant seeks certification for the Farmland as organic, Tenant shall bear all costs of obtaining the certification.

In Witness Whereof, the parties have executed and delivered this Agreement as of the date hereof.

Landlord:
Farmland Holding Co.
By: Justin Case /s
Justin Case, Vice-President

Tenant:
Stan Hatch /s
Stan Hatch

Farmer Stan submitted his first payment and hired LandTesters, Inc. to certify the land for growing organic food. The front forty acres received the organic certification but LandTesters unearthed a toxic waste dumpsite along the back ten acres of the farmland. The back ten acres cannot be certified organic within the next five years.

Both Farmer Stan and Farmland Holding Co. have hired attorneys to renegotiate the terms of the lease. You represent one of the two parties and are tasked with reaching a suitable agreement according to the additional needs of your client (as provided by your professor). Please record and sign the significant terms of your agreement. If you are unable to agree on terms, you and the opposing counsel are to jointly draft and sign a letter to your clients, describing the negotiation process and stating why you are unable to agree.

Points to Consider:

(1) In the contract, did either party assume the risk that the property would not be suitable for organic farming? What language are you relying on to support your answer?

(2) If the contract is silent on the question, are there any other circumstances that might lead a court to assign the risk to one of the parties?

(3) What are your client's alternative options and how motivated is your client to reach an agreement on this specific plot of land? What are the maximum and minimum amounts your client is willing to pay/receive for the farmland?

Term Sheet

Memorandum of Agreed Terms for the
Amendment to the Agricultural Lease:

1.

_____
Attorney for Stan Hatch
[Date]

_____
Attorney for Farmland Holding Co.
[Date]

CHAPTER NINE

Form Contracts &
Contracts of Adhesion
Restaurant Playground

YOUR FIRM REPRESENTS "Fast & Fun," a regional fast-food restaurant, known for their fry sauce, ice cream, and indoor playgrounds. Last year, following several high profile playground accidents, the restaurant vastly increased playground safety and began requiring parents sign a waiver before their children could enter the playgrounds. The "waiver" is a standard form contract, similar to the waivers required by the restaurant's competitors. The print is mostly ten-point font and important sections, about half of the agreement, are in bold or all-caps. Studies show almost no parents read the agreement with hot food on the table and a child screaming to play.

A national news team has recently broadcast unflattering stories on similar agreements used by the restaurant's competitors, highlighting difficult to read language and unexpected clauses. The restaurant's in house counsel has asked your firm to review the current waiver and suggest more appropriate language. Do not spend more than an hour or two on this assignment.

PLAYGROUND RELEASE

Whereas, I realize activities, not limited to standing, sitting, jumping, squatting, bending, and such forth, may present my child with opportunities for injury and or death. **Playground presents children with various opportunities for such activities.**

Whereas, I realize Restaurant owns, maintains, and provides use of Playground in accordance to written safety standards available by submitting a written request and two U.S. Dollars for shipping to: 123 Restaurant Management Drive, Blackacre USA. I hereby acknowledge the safety standards exceed adequacy.

NOW, THEREFORE, in consideration for access to the Synthetic Gymnastics PlayCenter located at a Restaurant location ("Playground"), the signee, hereby a parent or legal guardian of one or more minors to use Playground, does agree forthwith:

I will personally provide direct supervision of my child(ren) when engaged with Playground including maintaining a special radius not to exceed ten feet between myself and my child. **In the event of injury, I authorize Restaurant staff to provide first aid to myself and/or my child(ren) and/or to arrange medical transport.**

I will not hold Restaurant responsible for any injuries suffered by my child(ren) while using Playground, after exiting playground but before leaving Restaurant premises, or associated with foods consumed at Restaurant. I agree to RELEASE, DISCHARGE, INDEMNIFY, PROMISE NOT TO SUE AND TO SAVE AND HOLD HARMLESS Restaurant, its owners, officers, directors, contractors and employees, from any loss, liability, damage, or costs whatsoever arising out of or related to any loss, damage, or injury (including death) to me or my child(ren) arising out of or in anyway connected to use of Playground for any reason or cause.

I understand that this release and waiver of liability, assumption of risk, and hold harmless agreement is governed by the laws of the State of Blackacre, and is intended to be as broad and inclusive as is permitted by such law, and that, in the event any portion of this agreement is determined to be invalid, illegal, or unenforceable, the validity, legality, and enforceability of the balance of the agreement will not be affected or impaired in any way, and will continue to full legal force and effect. This release and waiver of liability is to be enforced and interpreted only by binding arbitration in Hawaii.

I HAVE READ THIS DOCUMENT AND AGREE TO ALL OF ITS TERMS. I UNDERSTAND IT IS A LEGALLY BINDING AGREEMENT AND WAIVES CERTAIN LEGAL RIGHTS OF MINE, INCLUDING, BUT NOT LIMITED TO A RELEASE, WAIVER, PROMISE NOT TO SUE AND A HOLD HARMLESS FOR ALL CLAIMS. THIS AGREEMENT SHALL BE BINDING UPON MYSELF, MY CHILD(REN), AND OUR ESTATE, SUCCESSORS AND ASSIGNS.

_____ _____

Signature   Date

Points to Consider

(1)   Forms such as this are often called "contracts of adhesion" because there is no realistic opportunity to negotiate the terms of the agreement. Such contracts are offered on a "take it or leave it basis." Despite the pejorative implications of the word "adhesion," form contracts such as this serve legitimate commercial purposes. What might they be?

(2) The parents signing this release have no realistic opportunity to review the contractual language with an attorney. In what ways should this fact affect how the form is drafted?

(3) In litigation involving serious injury or death, courts will sometimes hold form releases to be void as against public policy. What public policies are implicated in such cases?

(4) Although it is uncertain whether a form release such as this will be enforced, it is nevertheless a good idea for many businesses to ask their patrons to sign such a form. What other purpose besides protection from liability do such forms serve?

Playground Release Form

Think about using headings to organize your redraft of the release form. Some possible headings are:
• Acknowledgment of Playground Risks
• Obligation to Supervise
• Release of Liability
• Dispute Resolution

PLAYGROUND RELEASE

Playground Release Form, continued

_____   _____
Signature   Date

CHAPTER TEN

Capstone Exercise
Housing Issues

SOUTHERNSUN, INC. specializes in converting undeveloped desert land outside major cities in the southwestern United States into residential housing communities. They contract portions of the projects, like building roads, installing sewer systems, and constructing homes, to various specialized subcontractors.

ABC Framers, LLC, specializes in framing residential walls and roofs. ABC entered into a contract with SouthernSun to construct the walls and roof of a home on each of the sites in the Lizard Lake Subdivision in Boomtown, Blackacre, for $18,000 per site. When ABC arrived at each site, the previous subcontractor was to have poured a concrete floor, ABC would frame the walls and roof, the next subcontractor would install stucco and siding, and so on. The subcontractors were to follow each other from site to site until they had performed their portion of the project on each site in the subdivision. In this case, the Lizard Lakes Subdivision had 600 homes.

ABC incurred significant expenses mobilizing tools, equipment, and a labor force. They secured temporary housing in the Lizard Lakes area, acquired insurance, and declined to accept other lucrative contracts for the duration of the project. ABC completed 30 units before a housing crisis hit and building came to a standstill. The concrete subcontractor quit when the price of concrete rose and SouthernSun fired the stucco subcontractor for using drugs on the job site. Therefore, the next site was not ready for ABC to begin building and no one ever put stucco on the last house they framed. Eventually ABC brought their workers home and the two parties have been in a legal dispute since. Years later, the subdivision has not been finished and thousands of homes in neighboring subdivisions are vacant. Both parties agree the Lizard Lake subdivision is going to lose money; they just don't agree on who is responsible.

You will be assigned to represent either ABC or SouthernSun. Your assignment is in four parts. Your professor may assign one or more, or all, of the following:

Part I: Client Counseling

You have an hour to prepare for a meeting with your client, either ABC Framers or SouthernSun, to discuss how to resolve the dispute. Prepare a checklist of points to discuss at the meeting. Be sure to discuss issues of both liability and damages.

 ## Points to Consider:

What additional information would you like to know to answer their questions? How will you advise?

Client Counseling Memo

Your Name:

Client's Name & Name of Client Representative:

Date:

Client Goals:

Key Points to be Discussed:

Recommendations:

Part II: Advocacy

Using the template below, draft a Complaint either for ABC against
SouthernSun or for SouthernSun against ABC. (Review the Complaint
included in Chapter 6.) Your client has requested you do this in preparation for settlement negotiations. SouthernSun is incorporated in the
state of Delaware and has its principal place of business in Sun City,
Whiteacre. ABC is incorporated and has its principal place of business
in the state of Blackacre. Allocate no more than an hour or two to draft
the Complaint.

 Points to Consider:

(1) What, if any, factual inquiries must you undertake before drafting
the complaint?

(2) What will be the basis for your suit? Will it include more than one
cause of action?

(3) Why is this Complaint being filed in federal court as opposed to
state court?

Complaint

[Your name], Bar No. 777
Workhard & Longe
Attorney for Plaintiff
123 Main St.
Anywhere, Blackacre
Your.name@WLlaw.com
000.123.4567

IN THE UNITED STATES DISTRICT COURT
FOR THE SOUTHERN DISTRICT OF BLACKACRE

Plaintiff	)	COMPLAINT
v.	)	
	)	
	)	
Defendant.	)	

COMPLAINT

Plaintiff _____ alleges as follows:

PARTIES, JURISDICTION & VENUE

1. Plaintiff is a corporation incorporated under the laws of [Blackacre, or Delaware, as appropriate].

2. Defendant is [a Delaware corporation and does substantial business in Blackacre, or a Blackacre corporation, as appropriate].

3. This court has jurisdiction pursuant to 28 U.S.C. § 1331. The parties are diverse. Plaintiff seeks damages in excess of $75,000.

4. Venue is proper in the Southern District of the United States District Court of Blackacre as a substantial part of the events giving rise to the claim(s) occurred in this district.

[FIRST] CAUSE OF ACTION

5. _____

_____

_____

_____

_____

_____

_____

_____

_____

_____

WHEREFORE, Plaintiff demands judgment against Defendant for damages in an amount to be established at trial, an award of attorney's fees and costs, and such other relief as the court deems appropriate.

DATED this ___ day of _____, 20___

                                Workhard & Longe
                                Attorney for Plaintiff

                                By_____
                                [Your name], Bar No. 777
                                Workhard & Longe
                                123 Main St.
                                Anywhere, Blackacre

Part III: Negotiations

Facing prolonged litigation costs, mounting attorney fees, and an uncertain outcome, SouthernSun and ABC have instructed their attorneys to enter into settlement negotiations. Your professor will provide additional instructions. Record the essential terms on the form provided. If you are unable to reach an agreement, draft a memo to your client describing your negotiation strategy, how the negotiations proceeded, and recommendations for resolving the conflict with the opposing party.

 Points to Consider:

(1) Review the Supplement on Negotiation Strategy: what will be your strategy going into the settlement negotiations?

(2) The problem implies that only attorneys are going to be present at the settlement negotiations. What are the limits on what an attorney can or cannot agree to when representing a client in settlement negotiations?

Term Sheet Form

Term Sheet

_____

Attorney for Southern Sun

[Date]

_____

Attorney for ABC

[Date]

Part IV: Drafting

Draft a settlement agreement that incorporates the terms you
negotiated in the prior exercise or that your professor provides.
The "frame" of the contract is provided below. Consult Appendix A
for an introduction to contract drafting. Also, review the contracts or
parts of contracts included with earlier assignments for guidance.

 Points to Consider:

(1) Will the settlement agreement include an admission of fault
by either party?

(2) Will it include a confidentiality provision?

(3) How broadly or narrowly will the "claims" be defined?

Settlement Agreement

This **Settlement Agreement,** dated _____, 20__, is between ABC Framers, LLC, a Blackacre corporation ("ABC"), and SouthernSun, Inc., a Delaware corporation ("Sun").

[Background or Recitals, if any]

The parties agree as follows:

_____

_____

_____

_____

_____

_____

_____

_____

_____

_____

_____

_____

_____

_____

_____

_____

_____

_____

_____

_____

_____

_____

_____

To evidence the parties' agreement to this Agreement, they have executed and delivered it on the date set forth in the preamble.

BC Framers, LLC

By: _____, _____

[Name]   [Title]

SouthernSun, Inc.

By: _____, _____

[Name]   [Title]

APPENDIX A:

A Brief Introduction to Contract Drafting

To understand contract drafting[1], you should recognize that it involves two sets of ideas that together make up every contract. First, there are the organizational parts of a contract; second, there are contractual concepts, which are the different operative elements within the contract.

The Parts of a Contract

Like most legal documents, contracts follow a basic format. The "style" of a contract may differ widely from one law office to another, and the length and detail of a contract will vary greatly depending on how complicated the transaction is, but every contract contains at least some of the common contract parts. They are:

> The **"frame" of the contract**, consisting of the introductory sections at the beginning (the preamble, recitals (if any[2]), and words of agreement) and the signatory section at the end.

> A **definitions section** (optional; definitions may also be placed in the body of the contract as the need for them arises).

> The **business sections**, which include the subject of the contract (e.g., "Buyer shall purchase and Seller shall sell"), the consideration to be paid, closing information (if there is to be a closing; not all contracts involve closings), the factual representations made by each party and on which the other party is relying, and anything else that the parties are obligated or are given the discretion to do.

---

1 For further discussion of contract drafting, the following are recommended: Margaret Temple-Smith and Deborah E. Cupples, *Legal Drafting: Litigation Documents, Contracts, Legislation, and Wills* (2013); Tina L. Stark, *Drafting Contracts: How and Why Lawyers Do What They Do* (2007).

2 Recitals should be used sparingly and should never include substantive contract provisions, as some courts have held that recitals are not part of the parties' "contract" because they are placed before the words of agreement.

The **termination sections**, which set out how and under what circumstances the contract ends or can be terminated by one or both parties.

The **general provisions**, sometimes called the "boilerplate," which set out provisions for where to deliver notices, what law applies, whether the contract can be assigned or delegated, etc.

The Contractual Concepts

The parts of a contract make up the organization of the contract, but the contractual concepts consist of the operative language in a contract. They are the words that create contractual rights and obligations, are the basis for contractual liability or authority, and set out policies for regulating the contractual relationship. An easy way to think about the concepts is to associate them with verbs, or "actions." Just as every sentence must have a verb, every operative sentence in a contract contains at least one of these concepts. They are:

Declarations. A **declaration** sets policy for the contractual relationship. For example, a drafter uses a **declaration** to define a term, or to provide that New York law governs the agreement. A **declaration** does not create any obligation or liability. A **declaration** is signaled by the present tense of the verb "to be." This means that, because all definitions are declarations, they should be written in the present tense. E.g., "The Purchase Price is $25,000." Note that the definition does not obligate the purchaser to pay the purchase price; to do that, the drafter would use a **covenant**.

Covenants. A **covenant** obligates a party to do or refrain from doing something; it also creates a right to the obligated party's performance belonging to the other party. In other words, a **covenant** is a contractual promise. A **covenant** is signaled by the use of "shall."[3] "Buyer

---

3   It should be noted that the use of "shall" to signal a **covenant** is not subject to universal agreement. In some firms, a **covenant** is signaled by the use of "will;" in other firms, both "shall" and "will" (and sometimes "must") are used interchangeably. Best practice, however, is to use "shall" because, unlike "will" or "must," it

shall pay the Purchase Price" is an example of a **covenant. Covenants** are one of the three contractual concepts that are routinely studied in first year contracts classes (the other two being **representations** and **conditions,** as discussed below). First year law students read a number of cases construing and interpreting promissory language, that is, language creating a **covenant**.

Representations and Warranties. Technically, "**representations**" and "**warranties**" are not synonyms. Briefly, a "representation" can only be made with regard to past or present facts; the verb must be in the past or present tense. A "warranty" is a promise that a fact (usually regarding the condition of some thing) is true; unlike representations, warranties can extend into the future. E.g., "Seller warrants that the product is free of defects for a period of one year from purchase." The remedies for each also differ in some respects. However, for our purposes the difference between them is not crucial.

Together, representations and warranties can create liability on the part of the party making them if a fact is not as represented. For example, if an employee represents and warrants that she has earned a J.D. from State University and this is untrue, the employee could be liable in damages for misrepresentation and breach of warranty, or the false representation could result in a recession of the contract. First year contracts students typically study cases where one party is alleged to have misrepresented a fact and the other party is seeking damages or recession.

---

unambiguously signals an obligation. Conversely, "will" can be used to indicate futurity, as in, "The Landlord shall pay for re-painting the leased premises, but the Tenant may choose the color that the painter *will* use." In that sentence, "will" does not create any obligation on the part of the Landlord or the Tenant (and the painter is not a party to the Lease Agreement between them and so cannot be obligated under it); it merely indicates something that is going to occur in the future. Similarly, as discussed in the text, "must" can be used to signal a **condition** rather than a **covenant**. To avoid ambiguity, which is a central goal of contract drafting, it is best to use "shall" when drafting a **covenant**.

Discretionary Authority. A grant of **discretionary authority** gives a party the discretion to do or refrain from doing something, but does not obligate the party to do anything. A grant of **discretionary authority** is signaled by the use of "may." In the sentence, "The Landlord shall pay for re-painting the leased premises, but the Tenant may choose the color that the painter will use," the use of "shall" indicates the Landlord is obligated to pay (it creates a **covenant**), while the use of "may" indicates that the Tenant has the discretion to choose the color of the paint (it creates a **discretionary authority**).

Conditions. A **condition** is "an event, not certain to occur, which must occur ... before performance under a contract becomes due." (Restatement of Contracts 2d § 224.) **Conditions** are studied in first year contracts classes, both "express conditions," which are set out in the parties' agreement, and "implied conditions," which are read into the agreement by the court. As contract drafters, we are concerned only with express conditions. Of all the contract concepts, **conditions** are probably the trickiest to master, for at least four reasons. First of all, they never occur in isolation; a **condition** is always attached to an obligation (either a specific **covenant** or the contract as a whole) or a grant of **discretionary authority**.[4] Second, unlike the other contract concepts, the language signaling a **condition** can vary from contract to contract and even within a single contract. Third, the common law is not fond of **conditions** and, in cases of ambiguity, a judge often prefers to interpret the provision as creating a **covenant** instead of a **condition**. And finally, the failure of a **condition** does not, in and of itself, create any liability or right to damages; that is, a **condition** is never breached: it is either satisfied or it fails. The **condition** might "trigger" an obligation but it did not create the obligation; some other contract language did that. Similarly, the failure of a **condition** may have unpleasant consequences, such as allowing one party to terminate the contract, but there will never be a right to damages because

---

4 Occasionally, a **declaration** can be subject to a **condition** as well, but it will suffice for an introduction to drafting if you grasp the idea of an obligation (including a **covenant**) or a grant of **discretionary authority** being subject to a **condition**.

the **condition** failed to occur (unless a party also promised that the conditional "event" would occur, but that promise would have to be found in separate language creating a **covenant**).

A **condition** can be signaled by the use of phrases such as "if," "provided that," "in the event of," "unless," or "it is a condition of," as well as by the use of the verb "must." A common example of an obligation subject to a condition is found in many real estate purchase contracts, where the buyer's obligation to close on the purchase of the home is conditioned on the buyer obtaining financing. Obtaining financing is the "event, not certain to occur, which must occur" before the buyer becomes obligated to purchase.

The following is an example of a grant of **discretionary authority** subject to a **condition**: "If the Tenant fails to pay the Rent on or before the tenth day of each calendar month, the Landlord may impose a $25 late fee." Here, the Tenant's late payment is the "event, not certain to occur, which must occur" before the Landlord can exercise its **discretionary authority** to impose a late fee. (Note that the Landlord is not obligated to impose a late fee; it may or may not do so, at its discretion.) Moreover, assuming the Lease also obligated the Tenant to pay the rent on time (for example, it also included the provision "The Tenant shall pay the Rent on or before the tenth day of each calendar month"), the late payment would be both the **condition** triggering the Landlord's **discretionary authority** to impose a late fee *and* a breach of the Tenant's promise or **covenant**, which would give the Landlord a separate right to damages. (Typically, the damages would be the unpaid rent plus interest.)

As stated above, every provision in a contract falls into one of the above categories of contract concepts, depending on what the provision seeks to accomplish:

- Definition or statement of policy = declaration.
- Obligation or promise to do something = covenant.
- Fact to be relied upon = representation and warranty.
- Option to do something = discretionary authority.
- Triggering event = condition.

APPENDIX B
Selected Provisions of the Model Rules
of Professional Conduct

Rule 1.0   Terminology

Rule 1.1   Competence

Rule 1.2   Scope of Representation and Allocation of Authority Between Client and Lawyer

Rule 1.4   Communication

Rule 1.6   Confidentiality

Rule 1.7   Conflict of Interest

Rule 1.13   Organization as Client

Rule 1.16   Declining or Terminating Representation

Rule 1.18   Duties to Prospective Client

Rule 2.1   Advisor

Rule 3.1   Meritorious Claims and Contentions

Rule 3.3   Candor Toward the Tribunal

Rule 3.4   Fairness to Opposing Party and Counsel

Rule 4.1   Truthfulness in Statement to Others

Rule 4.3   Dealing with Unrepresented Person

Rule 5.2   Responsibilities of a Subordinate Lawyer

Rule 6.1   Voluntary Pro Bono Publico Service

Rule 8.4   Misconduct

Rule 1.0 Terminology

(a) "Belief" or "believes" denotes that the person involved actually supposed the fact in question to be true. A person's belief may be inferred from circumstances.

(b) "Confirmed in writing," when used in reference to the informed consent of a person, denotes informed consent that is given in writing by the person or a writing that a lawyer promptly transmits to the person confirming an oral informed consent. See paragraph (e) for the definition of "informed consent." If it is not feasible to obtain or transmit the writing at the time the person gives informed consent, then the lawyer must obtain or transmit it within a reasonable time thereafter.

(c) "Firm" or "law firm" denotes a lawyer or lawyers in a law partnership, professional corporation, sole proprietorship or other association authorized to practice law; or lawyers employed in a legal services organization or the legal department of a corporation or other organization.

(d) "Fraud" or "fraudulent" denotes conduct that is fraudulent under the substantive or procedural law of the applicable jurisdiction and has a purpose to deceive.

(e) "Informed consent" denotes the agreement by a person to a proposed course of conduct after the lawyer has communicated adequate information and explanation about the material risks of and reasonably available alternatives to the proposed course of conduct.

(f) "Knowingly," "known," or "knows" denotes actual knowledge of the fact in question. A person's knowledge may be inferred from circumstances.

(g) "Partner" denotes a member of a partnership, a shareholder in a law firm organized as a professional corporation, or a member of an association authorized to practice law.

(h) Reasonable" or "reasonably" when used in relation to conduct by a lawyer denotes the conduct of a reasonably prudent and competent lawyer.

(i) "Reasonable belief" or "reasonably believes" when used in reference to a lawyer denotes that the lawyer believes the matter in question and that the circumstances are such that the belief is reasonable.

(j) "Reasonably should know" when used in reference to a lawyer denotes that a lawyer of reasonable prudence and competence would ascertain the matter in question.

(k) "Screened" denotes the isolation of a lawyer from any participation in a matter through the timely imposition of procedures within a firm that are reasonably adequate under the circumstances to protect information that the isolated lawyer is obligated to protect under the Rules or other law.

(l) "Substantial" when used in reference to degree or extent denotes a material matter of clear and weighty importance.

(m) "Tribunal" denotes a court, an arbitrator in a binding arbitration proceeding or a legislative body, administrative agency or other body acting in an adjudicative capacity. A legislative body, administrative agency or other body acts in an adjudicative capacity when a neutral official, after the presentation of evidence or legal argument by a party or parties, will render a binding legal judgment directly affecting a party's interests in a particular matter.

(n) "Writing" or "written" denotes a tangible or electronic record of a communication or representation, including handwriting, typewriting, printing, photostating, photography, audio or videorecording, and electronic communications. A "signed" writing includes an electronic sound, symbol or process attached to or logically associated with a writing and executed or adopted by a person with the intent to sign the writing.

Rule 1.1 Competence

A lawyer shall provide competent representation to a client. Competent representation requires the legal knowledge, skill, thoroughness and preparation reasonably necessary for the representation.

Rule 1.2 Scope of Representation And Allocation of Authority Between Client and Lawyer

(a) Subject to paragraph (c) and (d), a lawyer shall abide by a client's decisions concerning the objectives of representation and, as required by Rule 1.4, shall consult with the client as to the means by which they are to be pursued. A lawyer may take such action on behalf of the client as is impliedly authorized to carry out the representation. A lawyer shall abide by a client's decision whether to settle a matter...

(b) A lawyer's representation of a client, including representation by appointment, does not constitute an endorsement of the client's political, economic, social or moral views or activities.

(c) A lawyer may limit the scope of the representation if the limitation is reasonable under the circumstances and the client gives informed consent.

(d) A lawyer shall not counsel a client to engage, or assist a client, in conduct that the lawyer knows is criminal or fraudulent, but a lawyer may discuss the legal consequences of any proposed course of conduct with a client and may counsel or assist a client to make a good faith effort to determine the validity, scope, meaning or application of the law.

Rule 1.4 Communication

(a) A lawyer shall:

    (1) promptly inform the client of any decision or circumstance with respect to which the client's informed consent, as defined in Rule 1.0(e), is required by these Rules;

    (2) reasonably consult with the client about the means by which the client's objectives are to be accomplished;

    (3) keep the client reasonably informed about the status of the matter;

    (4) promptly comply with reasonably requests for information; and

    (5) consult with the client about any relevant limitation on the lawyer's conduct when the lawyer knows that the client expects assistance not permitted by the Rules of Professional Conduct or other law.

(b) A lawyer shall explain a matter to the extent reasonably necessary to permit the client to make informed decisions regarding the representation.

Rule 1.6 Confidentiality of Information

(a) A lawyer shall not reveal information relating to the representation of a client unless the client gives informed consent, the disclosure is impliedly authorized in order to carry out the representation or the disclosure is permitted by paragraph (b).

(b) A lawyer may reveal information relating to the representation of a client to the extent the lawyer reasonably believes necessary:

   (1) to prevent reasonably certain death or substantial bodily harm;

   (2) to prevent the client from committing a crime or fraud that is reasonably certain to result in substantial injury to the financial interests or property of another and in furtherance of which the client has used or is using the lawyer's services;

   (3) to prevent, mitigate or rectify substantial injury to the financial interests or property or another that is reasonably certain to result or has resulted from the client's commission of a crime or fraud in furtherance of which the client has used the lawyer's services;

   (4) to secure legal advice about the lawyer's compliance with these Rules;

   (5) to establish a claim or defense on behalf of the lawyer in a controversy between the lawyer and the client, to establish a defense to a criminal charge or civil claim against the lawyer based upon conduct in which the client was involved, or to respond to allegations in any proceeding concerning the lawyer's representation of the client;

   (6) to comply with other law or a court order; or

   (7) to detect and resolve conflicts of interest arising from the lawyer's change of employment or from changes in the composition or ownership of a firm, but only if the revealed information would not compromise the attorney-client privilege or otherwise prejudice the client.

(c) A lawyer shall make reasonable efforts to prevent the inadvertent or unauthorized disclosure of, or unauthorized access to, information relating to the representation of a client.

Rule 1.7 Conflict of Interest: Current Clients

(a) Except as provided in paragraph (b), a lawyer shall not represent a client if the representation involves a concurrent conflict of interest.

A concurrent conflict of interest exists if:

(1) the representation of one client will be directly adverse to another client; or

(2) there is a significant risk that the representation of one or more clients will be materially limited by the lawyer's responsibilities to another client, a former client or a third person or by a personal interest of the lawyer.

(b) Notwithstanding the existence of a concurrent conflict of interest under paragraph (a), a lawyer may represent a client if:

(1) the lawyer reasonably believes that the lawyer will be able to provide competent and diligent representation to each affected client;

(2) the representation is not prohibited by law;

(3) the representation does not involve the assertion of a claim by one client against another client represented by the lawyer in the same litigation or other proceeding before a tribunal; and

(4) each affected client gives informed consent, confirmed in writing.

Rule 1.13 Organization as Client

(a) A lawyer employed or retained by an organization represents the organization acting through its duly authorized constituents.

(b) If a lawyer for an organization knows that an officer, employee or other person associated with the organization is engaged in action, intends to act or refuses to act in a matter related to the representation that is a violation of a legal obligation to the organization, or a violation of law that reasonably might be imputed to the organization, and that is likely to result in substantial injury to the organization, then the lawyer shall proceed as is reasonably necessary in the best interest of the organization. Unless the lawyer reasonably believes that it is not necessary in the best interest of the organization to do so, the lawyer shall refer the matter to higher authority in the organization, including, if warranted by the circumstances to the highest authority that can act on behalf of the organization as determined by applicable law.

(c) Except as provided in paragraph (d), if
  (1) despite the lawyer's effort in accordance with paragraph (b) the highest authority that can act on behalf of the organization insists upon or fails to address in a timely and appropriate manner an action, or a refusal to act, that is clearly a violation of law, and
  (2) the lawyer reasonably believes that the violation is reasonably certain to result in substantial injury to the organization, then the lawyer may reveal information relating to the representation whether or not Rule 1.6 permits such disclosure, but only if and to the extent the lawyer reasonably believes necessary to prevent substantial injury to the organization.

(d) Paragraph(c) shall not apply with respect to information relating to a lawyer's representation of an organization to investigate an alleged violation of law, or to defend the organization or an officer, employee or other constituent associated with the organization against a claim arising out of an alleged violation of law.

(e) A lawyer who reasonably believes that he or she has been discharged because of the lawyer's actions taken pursuant to paragraphs (b) or (c), or who withdraws under circumstances that require or permit the lawyer to take action under either of those paragraphs, shall proceed as the lawyer reasonably believes necessary to assure that the organization's highest authority is informed of the lawyer's discharge or withdrawal.

(f) In dealing with an organization's directors, officers, employees, members, shareholders or other constituents, a lawyer shall explain the identity of the client when the lawyer knows or reasonably should know that the organization's interests are adverse to those of the constituents with whom the lawyer is dealing.

(g) A lawyer representing an organization may also represent any of its directors, officers, employees, members, shareholders or other constituents, subject to the provisions of Rule 1.7. If the organization's consent to the dual representation is required by Rule 1.7, the consent shall be given by an appropriate official of the organization other than the individual who is to be represented, or by the shareholders.

Rule 1.16

Declining Or Terminating Representation

(a) Except as stated in paragraph (c), a lawyer shall not represent a client or, where representation has commenced, shall withdraw from the representation of a client if:

    (1) the representation will result in violation of the Rules of Professional Conduct or other law;

    (2) the lawyer's physical or mental condition materially impairs the lawyer's ability to represent the client; or

    (3) the lawyer is discharged.

(b) Except as stated in paragraph (c), a lawyer may withdraw from representing a client if:

    (1) withdrawal can be accomplished without material adverse effect on the interests of the client;

    (2) the client persists in a course of action involving the lawyer's services that the lawyer reasonably believes is criminal or fraudulent;

    (3) the client has used the lawyer's services to perpetrate a crime or fraud;

    (4) the client insists upon taking action that the lawyer consid-
       ers repugnant or with which the lawyer has a fundamental
       disagreement;

    (5) the client fails substantially to fulfill an obligation to the lawyer
       regarding the lawyer's services and has been given reasonable
       warning that the lawyer will withdraw unless the obligation is
       fulfilled;

    (6) the representation will result in an unreasonable financial
       burden on the lawyer or has been rendered unreasonably
       difficult by the client; or

    (7) other good cause for withdrawal exists.

(c) A lawyer must comply with applicable law requiring notice to
or permission of a tribunal when terminating a representation.
When ordered to do so by a tribunal, a lawyer shall continue
representation notwithstanding good cause for terminating the
representation.

(d) Upon termination of representation, a lawyer shall take steps to the
extent reasonably practicable to protect a client's interests, such
as giving reasonable notice to the client, allowing time for employment of other counsel, surrendering papers and property to which
the client is entitled and refunding any advance payment of fee
or expense that has not been earned or incurred. The lawyer may
retain papers relating to the client to the extent permitted by law.

Rule 1.18 Duties to Prospective Client

(a) A person who consults with a lawyer about the possibility of form-
ing a client-lawyer relationship with respect to a matter is a prospective client.

(b) Even when no client-lawyer relationship ensues, a lawyer who has
learned information from a prospective client shall not use or reveal that information, except as Rule 1.9 would permit with respect
to information of a former client.

(c) A lawyer subject to paragraph (b) shall not represent a client with interests materially adverse to those of a prospective client in the same or a substantially related matter if the lawyer received information from the prospective client that could be significantly harmful to that person in the matter, except as provided in paragraph (d). If a lawyer is disqualified from representation under this paragraph, no lawyer in a firm with which that lawyer is associated may knowingly undertake or continue representation in such a matter, except as provided in paragraph (d).

(d) When the lawyer has received disqualifying information as defined in paragraph (c), representation is permissible if:

    (1)   both the affected client and the prospective client have given informed consent, confirmed in writing, or:

    (2)   the lawyer who received the information took reasonable measures to avoid exposure to more disqualifying information than was reasonably necessary to determine whether to represent the prospective client; and

        (i) the disqualified lawyer is timely screened from any participation in the matter and is apportioned no part of the fee therefrom; and

        (ii) written notice is promptly given to the prospective client.

Rule 2.1 Advisor

In representing a client, a lawyer shall exercise independent professional judgment and render candid advice. In rendering advice, a lawyer may refer not only to law but to other consideration such as moral, economic, social and political factors, that may be relevant to the client's situation.

Rule 3.1 Meritorious Claims and Contentions

A lawyer shall not bring or defend a proceeding, or assert or controvert an issue therein, unless there is a basis in law and fact for doing so that is not frivolous, which includes a good faith argument for an extension, modification or reversal of existing law...

• MODEL RULES OF PROFESSIONAL CONDUCT

Rule 3.3 Candor Toward the Tribunal

(a) A lawyer shall not knowingly:

(1) make a false statement of fact or law to a tribunal or fail to correct a false statement of material fact or law previously made to the tribunal by the lawyer;

(2) fail to disclosure to the tribunal legal authority in the controlling jurisdiction known to the lawyer to be directly adverse to the position of the client and not disclosed by apposing counsel; or

(3) offer evidence that the lawyer knows to be false. If a lawyer, the lawyer's client, or a witness called by the lawyer, has offered material evidence and the lawyer comes to know of its falsity, the lawyer shall take reasonable remedial measures, including, if necessary, disclosure to the tribunal. A lawyer may refuse to offer evidence, other than the testimony of a defendant in a criminal matter, that the lawyer reasonably believes is false.

(b) A lawyer who represents a client in an adjudicative proceeding and who knows that a person intends to engage, is engaging or has engaged in criminal or fraudulent conduct related to the proceeding shall take reasonable remedial measures, including, if necessary, disclosure to the tribunal.

(c) The duties stated in paragraphs (a) and (b) continue to the conclusion of the proceeding, and apply even if compliance requires disclosure of information otherwise protected by Rule 1.6.

(d) In an ex parte proceeding, a lawyer shall inform the tribunal of all material facts known to the lawyer that will enable the tribunal to make an informed decision, whether or not the facts are adverse.

Rule 3.4 Fairness to Opposing Party and Counsel

A lawyer shall not:

(a) unlawfully obstruct another party's access to evidence or unlawfully alter, destroy or conceal a document or other material having potential evidentiary value. A lawyer shall not counsel or assist another person to do any such act;

(b) falsify evidence, counsel or assist a witness to testify falsely, or offer an inducement to a witness that is prohibited by law;

(c) knowingly disobey an obligation under the rules of a tribunal except for an open refusal based on an assertion that no valid obligation exists;

(d) in pretrial procedure, make a frivolous discovery request or fail to make reasonably diligent effort to comply with a legally proper discovery request by an opposing party;

(e) in trial, allude to any matter that the lawyer does not reasonably believe is relevant or that will not be supported by admissible evidence, assert personal knowledge of facts in issue except when testifying as a witness, or state a personal opinion as to the justness of a cause, the credibility of a witness, the culpability of a civil litigant or the guilt or innocence of an accused; or

(f) request a person other than a client to refrain from voluntarily giving relevant information to another party unless:

   (1) the person is a relative or an employee or other agent of a client, and

   (2) the lawyer reasonably believes that the person's interests will not be adversely affected by refraining from giving such information.

Rule 4.1 Truthfulness In Statements to Others

In the course of representing a client a lawyer shall not knowingly:

(a) make a false statement of material fact or law to a third person; or

(b) fail to disclose a material fact to a third person when disclosure is necessary to avoid assisting a criminal or fraudulent act by a client, unless disclosure is prohibited by Rule 1.6.

Rule 4.3 Dealing With Unrepresented Person

In dealing on behalf of a client with a person who is not represented by counsel, a lawyer shall not state or imply that the lawyer is disinterested. When the lawyer knows or reasonably should know that the unrepresented person misunderstands the lawyer's role in the matter, the lawyer shall make reasonable efforts to correct the misunderstanding. The lawyer shall not give legal advice to an unrepresented person, other than the advice to secure counsel, if the lawyer knows or reasonably should know that the interests of such a person are or have a reasonable possibility of being in conflict with the interests of the client.

Rule 5.2 Responsibilities of a Subordinate Lawyer

(a) A lawyer is bound by the Rules of Professional Conduct notwithstanding that the lawyer acted at the direction of another person.

(b) A subordinate lawyer does not violate the Rules of Professional Conduct if that lawyer acts in accordance with a supervisory lawyer's reasonable resolution of an arguable question of professional duty.

Rule 6.1 Voluntary Pro Bono Publico Service

Every lawyer has a professional responsibility to provide legal services to those unable to pay. A lawyer should aspire to render at least (50) hours of pro bono publico legal services per year. In fulfilling this responsibility, the lawyer should:

(a) provide a substantial majority of the (50) hours of legal services without fee or expectation of fee to:

    (1) persons of limited means or

    (2) charitable, religious, civic, community, governmental and educational organizations in matters that are designed primarily to address the needs of persons of limited means; and

(b) provide any additional services through:

    (1) delivery of legal services at no fee or substantially reduced fee to individuals, groups or organizations seeking to secure or protect civil rights, civil liberties or public rights, or charitable, religious, civic, community, governmental and educational organizations in matters in furtherance of their organizational purposes, where the payment of standard legal fees would significantly deplete the organization's economic resources or would be otherwise inappropriate;

    (2) delivery of legal services at a substantially reduced fee to persons of limited means; or

    (3) participation in activities for improving the law, the legal system or the legal profession.

In addition, a lawyer should voluntarily contribute financial support to organizations that provide legal services to persons of limited means.

Rule 8.4 Misconduct

It is professional misconduct for a lawyer to:

(a) violate or attempt to violate the Rules of Professional Conduct, knowingly assist or induce another to do so, or do so through the acts of another;

(b) commit a criminal act that reflects adversely on the lawyer's honesty, trustworthiness or fitness as a lawyer in other respects;

(c) engage in conduct involving dishonesty, fraud, deceit or misrepresentation;

(d) engage in conduct that is prejudicial to the administration of justice;

(e) state or imply an ability to influence improperly a government agency or official or to achieve results by means that violate the Rules of Professional Conduct or other law; or

(f) knowingly assist a judge or judicial officer in conduct that is a violation of applicable rules of judicial conduct or other law.

APPENDIX C: Time Sheets

Attorney:
Client:
Billing No.

DATE	DESCRIPTION	TIME

APPENDIX C: Time Sheets

Attorney:
Client:
Billing No.

DATE	DESCRIPTION	TIME

APPENDIX C: Time Sheets

Attorney:

Client:

Billing No.

DATE	DESCRIPTION	TIME

APPENDIX C: Time Sheets

Attorney:
Client:
Billing No.

DATE	DESCRIPTION	TIME

APPENDIX C: Time Sheets

Attorney:
Client:
Billing No.

DATE	DESCRIPTION	TIME

APPENDIX C: Time Sheets

Attorney:
Client:
Billing No.

DATE	DESCRIPTION	TIME